W9-DAY-944

Main June 2013

Prickly Plants
Stuck!

by Ellen Lawrence

Consultants:

Suzy Gazlay, MA
Recipient, Presidential Award for Excellence in Science Teaching

Dr. Robin Wall Kimmerer
Professor of Environmental and Forest Biology
SUNY College of Environmental Science and Forestry, Syracuse, New York

Kimberly Brenneman, PhD
National Institute for Early Education Research, Rutgers University
New Brunswick, New Jersey

BEARPORT
PUBLISHING

New York, New York

Credits

Cover, © Konstantnin/Shutterstock and © Riegscker/Shutterstock and © Joe Belanger/Shutterstock; 3L, © bg_knight/Shutterstock; 3R, © Stefan Auth/Imagebroker/FLPA; 4–5, © Marketa Mark/Shutterstock and © Blue Ice/ShutterStock and © GTW/Imagebroker/FLPA5; 6, © Bragin Alexey/Shutterstock; 6–7, © EuToch/Shutterstock; 8, © Ingo Arndt/Minden Pictures/FLPA; 9, © Tim Fitzharris/Minden Pictures/FLPA; 10, © Annavee/Shutterstock; 11, © Jayne Chapman/Shutterstock; 12, © Lagui/Shutterstock; 13, © Carr Clifton/Minden Pictures/FLPA; 14, © Sergei Devyatkin/Shutterstock; 15TR, © Greg Hume/Wikipedia Creative Commons; 15B, © Laurin Rinder/Shutterstock; 16, © Winfried Wisniewski/FLPA; 17, © Tui De Roy/Minden Pictures/FLPA; 18, © Mark Moffett/Minden Pictures/FLPA; 19, © Mark Moffett/Minden Pictures/FLPA; 20BL, © Kokhanchikov/Shutterstock; 20R, © Dr. Keith Wheeler/Science Photo Library; 21, © Gerard Lacz/FLPA; 22, © Ruby Tuesday Books Ltd.; 23TL, © Regien Paassen/Shutterstock; 23TC, © Villiers Steyn/Shutterstock; 23TR, © Filipe B. Varela/Shutterstock; 23BL, © Max Topchii/Shutterstock; 23BC, © alexnika/Shutterstock; 23BR, © Laurin Rinder/Shutterstock.

Publisher: Kenn Goin
Editorial Director: Adam Siegel
Creative Director: Spencer Brinker
Design: Elaine Wilkinson
Photo Researcher: Ruby Tuesday Books Ltd

Library of Congress Cataloging-in-Publication Data

Lawrence, Ellen, 1967–
  Prickly plants : stuck! / by Ellen Lawrence.
     p. cm. — (Plant-ology)
  Includes bibliographical references and index.
  ISBN 978-1-61772-588-3 (library binding) — ISBN 1-61772-588-9 (library binding)
  1. Prickles—Juvenile literature. 2. Plant defenses—Juvenile literature. I. Title.
  QK650.L39 2013
  581.4'7—dc23
                            2012014336

For more information, write to Bearport Publishing Company, Inc., 45 West 21st Street, Suite 3B, New York, New York 10010. Printed in the United States of America.

10 9 8 7 6 5 4 3 2 1

Contents

A Deer's Dinner

A hungry deer in a desert is looking for some food.

It spots a large juicy cactus—but it doesn't dare take a bite.

Why?

The cactus has a way to make sure it doesn't end up as the deer's dinner.

A cactus is a type of plant that can survive in hot, dry places. Most cactuses, or cacti, grow in rocky or sandy **deserts**.

Why do you think the deer won't eat the cactus?

4

cactus

Prickly Protection

Plants can't move away from animals that want to eat them.

So some plants, such as cacti, have sharp prickles that are painful to touch or eat.

The prickles on a cactus are called **spines**.

Animals don't try to eat a cactus because the sharp spines would poke them.

spines

cactus

A Thirsty Cactus

The hot deserts where prickly cacti grow get very little rain.

When it does rain, these plants suck up as much water as they can through their **roots**.

Then they store the water they need in their thick, fleshy stems—sometimes for years!

A fully grown saguaro (suh-WAH-ruh) cactus can weigh as much as an elephant.

That's because it has so much water stored in its main stem and smaller stems, called arms.

saguaro cactus spine

The saguaro cactus spines in this photograph are life-size! Use a ruler to find out how long they are.

saguaro cactus

arm

stem

Saguaro cacti
can grow to be 50
feet (15 m) tall. It takes
them about 125 years to
grow this high. They
may live for around
200 years.

Don't Eat! Don't Drink!

Cacti don't need protection just from animals looking for a meal.

They also need protection from animals that want to get a drink.

A cactus's fleshy stem might be filled with gallons of water.

Eating the juicy plant would be a good way for a thirsty animal to get a drink.

Having spines helps the plant protect the water it has stored up.

spines

a stem filled with water

barrel cactus stem

A large barrel cactus can store enough water in its stem to last for more than five years.

Spines for Shade

Being prickly helps cacti survive in another important way—it keeps them cool.

For example, a teddy bear cholla (CHOI-yuh) cactus has thousands of prickly spines.

When the sun shines on a spine, it makes a little cooling shadow.

Together the spines make lots of shade and help the plant stay cool.

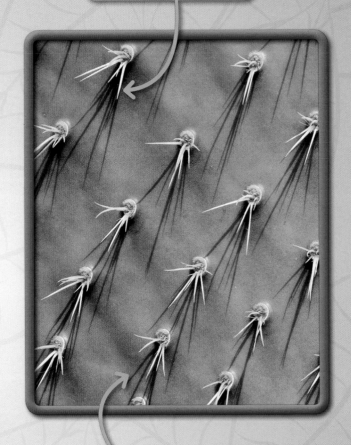

prickly pear spine

shadow

Which of the cacti in the book do you like the best? Describe what your favorite cactus looks like.

teddy bear
cholla cactus

spines

The teddy
bear cholla gets
its name because
its stems are so thickly
covered with spines that
the spines look like
the fur of a fuzzy
teddy bear.

13

Prickly Thorns

Some plants have **thorns** to stop animals from eating them.

Thorns are hard, pointed parts of a plant's stem.

Rosebushes have sharp thorns to stop animals from eating their sweet-smelling flowers.

This is important because flowers make seeds that will grow into new plants.

rose

thorns

14

Thorns can be small, like the hundreds of prickles on a rose stem. They can also be long and thick, like the six-inch-long (15-cm-long) thorns on a honey locust tree.

honey locust tree thorn

thorn

close-up photo of a rose stem

A Giraffe's Dinner

In Africa, thorny acacia (uh-KAY-shuh) trees grow on dry **grasslands** where very little rain falls.

Not many plants can live there, but there are lots of hungry plant-eating animals.

The acacia trees have long thorns to stop animals from eating their leaves.

The trees' protective thorns don't work against giraffes, though.

Giraffes have very long tongues that can bend around the thorns to grab the leaves!

The umbrella acacia tree gets its name from the shape of its branches and leaves. The tree grows two types of thorns—long straight ones and short hooked ones.

umbrella acacia tree

giraffe

acacia tree thorns

17

Thorns as Homes

Thorns aren't the only way that one kind of acacia tree protects itself.

The whistling acacia tree also gets help from stinging ants.

The ants make their homes in the rounded part of the tree's thorns.

They eat a sweet liquid, called sap, which oozes from the tree's leaves.

If another animal tries to eat the leaves, the ants sting its tongue and mouth.

whistling acacia tree

monkey

ant home

The whistling acacia's thorns have little holes where the ants go in and out. When the wind blows over the holes, the thorns make a whistling noise. That's how the trees got their name.

whistling acacia tree thorn

hole for going in and out

ant

Don't Touch!

There's a plant that has tiny prickly hairs to protect itself—a stinging nettle.

If an animal touches the hairs, they break off and get stuck in the animal's skin.

Then the hairs pump a stinging liquid into the skin.

Whether a plant has spines, thorns, or stinging hairs, these prickles say the same thing—don't touch!

close-up photo of stinging nettle hairs

stem

stinging nettle

land iguana

If there is no other food around, some kinds of animals will eat prickly plants. For example, land iguanas eat prickly pears—including the spines!

prickly pear

Science Lab

Give a prickly show and tell!

Make a model of a prickly cactus to show how the plant's spines help it survive.

Making a Cactus

1. Use green modeling clay to make the stems of your cactus.
2. Place your cactus in a flowerpot filled with sand or garden soil to help it stand up.
3. Push toothpicks into the model to give the cactus spines.

Present your model to your friends, family, or teacher.

Explain how a cactus's spines protect it from being eaten by animals.

Stand the cactus in a sunny place and check to see if the spines make shadows on the plant's stems.

Explain that these shadows help keep a cactus cool in its hot desert home.

Science Words

deserts (DEZ-urts) dry areas with few plants and little rainfall; deserts are often covered with sand or rocks

grasslands (GRASS-landz) hot, dry places with a lot of grass and small plants; only a few trees and bushes grow there

roots (ROOTS) underground parts of plants that take in nutrients and water from the soil; roots spread out in the soil to hold a plant in place

spines (SPYENZ) thin, spiky parts of a cactus that protect the plant from being eaten by animals

stems (STEMZ) upright parts of a plant that connect the roots to the leaves and flowers

thorns (THORNZ) hard, pointed parts of a plant's stem

Index

Read More

Gould, Margee. *Prickly Plants (The Strangest Plants on Earth).* New York: PowerKids Press (2012).

Maurer, Tracy. *What's in a Cactus?* Vero Beach, FL: Rourke (2011).

Sill, Cathryn. *Deserts (About Habitats).* Atlanta, GA: Peachtree Publishers (2007).

Learn More Online

To learn more about prickly plants, visit
www.bearportpublishing.com/Plant-ology

About the Author

Ellen Lawrence lives in the United Kingdom. Her favorite books to write are those about nature and animals. In fact, the first book Ellen bought for herself, when she was six years old, was the story of a gorilla named Patty Cake that was born in New York's Central Park Zoo.